The Object-Oriented Paradigm

The basics you need to know

Mariano Pagés

Table of Contents

Introduction	4
What are the objects?	8
The Object-Oriented Paradigm	12
What's inside the object paradigm?	17
Object	18
Attribute	22
Method	22
Message	22
Encapsulation	22
Information hiding	23
Class	24
Instance	29
Putting it all together: Objects, classes and messages	30
Abstraction	34
Inheritance	42
Abstract Class	44
Class Hierarchy	48
How do you run a method?	49
Polymorphism	50
Dynamic Linking	53
A universe of objects	55
How to solve problems by thinking about objects	56
The family tree	58
Object collections	68
Arrangements of objects	70

Dictionaries	72
Bags	73
Sets	76
Applying what we learned	78
Example 1: Integers from different bases	78
Example 2: Supermarket receipt	81
Example 3: The video rental store	86
Relationships between classes	91
Aggregation	92
Composition	93
Conclusions	94

Introduction

If your goal is to understand what the object-oriented paradigm is, what its ideas and foundations are, this is your book. On the other hand, if you want to learn object oriented design and analysis methodologies, or learn a good programming language in depth, you won't find those topics here, however, you should read this first anyway.

If you arrived here, you may be interested in the programming universe, or perhaps you have already become involved with it, studying formally or being self-taught. You may even have programmed in some languages.

Today the offer of programming languages is very rich. There is, however, a rather limited set of languages that I could call "blockbuster", which have a very high level of acceptance and popularity. However, this fame may be short lived, so investing time in learning them in detail may not be the best use of your time.

In my book "Algorithms at your fingertips", I referred to the difficulty of finding texts that teach problem solving, regardless of programming languages. When we learn to program, the nucleus of the matter is exactly, to learn to solve problems.

With the Object paradigm something similar happens. Exist many and very good books that teach to program using some language in particular, but the nucleus of this problem is found exactly in to understand what is the object-oriented programming and, in that way through a few concepts, to achieve to capture the essence of these languages and the way of thinking that underlies behind them. These concepts are found defined in the set of ideas contained in the paradigm of objects.

If we divide the engineering world into concepts on the one hand, and tools on the other, what you will find in this book is the first ones. However, trying to use the tools without fully understanding the set of ideas that motivated their construction can be the path more difficult.

For example, most people find it easier to drive a car with a manual gearbox if we understand the basics of its operation. What the gearbox is for, what the clutch is, how the brakes work, are all general and essential concepts. Once understood, when we get into a car, even if we have never driven it, we will know how to do it, at least in theory. We will know, for example, that we cannot stop it without pressing the clutch or putting it into neutral. Not only will we know to do that, but we will also **know why**. Then each car will have its own particularities according to its equipment, such as a cruise control. However, by understanding the essence of the general operation of the vehicle, we can imagine how it works and thus use it more efficiently.

Going back to the object-oriented programming, here you will find those fundamentals, which will allow you to better understand how each language implements them.

When it is necessary to incorporate some example, I will use a language without syntactic rigor based on Smalltalk, since it is one of those that better interprets the essence of the object oriented programming.

Speaking about my experience in particular, I had my first contact with Smalltalk in 1988, in my last year of college. In those years the exercises were solved using Pascal, a very good language to learn structured programming. Nevertheless, for some reason that I don't remember, a Smalltalk V diskette fell to my hands, that took me to the world of the objects, and it captivated me more than thirty years ago.

In all these years many object-oriented languages appeared. Some have even disappeared. The way the ideas of the paradigm are interpreted varies from one to another. However, they remain unchanged, and it is my interest that you learn about them through these pages.

It is my desire also, that the way of thinking that is behind this way of programming captivates you as much as it does me, or at least helps you to understand it, turning this set of ideas as part of your knowledge.

What are the objects?

It is clear that when we analyze the observable and apparent truth we find innumerable objects, and this we can affirm without having a formal definition of what an object is, since we all have an idea of what it is. We will see at once, that when we try to give it a definition, even more objects will appear before our eyes and thoughts.

Trying to define what an object is, the result is not as easy as it seems. Try, for example, to define what a "thing" is without using the word "thing". Not easy, isn't it?

Without taking a dictionary, I will try to define as clearly as possible, what is an object when we think about object-oriented programming.

"An object is any observable entity that has physical or imaginary existence, that has a set of relevant attributes or characteristics, and has a certain behavior within a limited reality.

In short, we can say that absolutely everything we can perceive is an object. However, we must analyze each part of the definition for the ideas that arise from it.

When we speak of "physical or imaginary existence", we surely must add to the idea of object that we may have had as children, things that are not tangible. For example, a bank account might be an object in a certain context, yet it does not have a physical existence. We can't put it in a cardboard box and wrap it up as a gift. Nor can we go to the bank and ask for our account because we want to take it home. But, anyway, it does exist.

While we talk and assume that there are objects with physical existence among us, such as an appliance or a person. If we go to the other extreme, all objects actually have an imaginary existence. No matter how real an object may seem, we always observe an idea we get from it. When we have an appliance in front of our eyes we will surely focus on some relevant characteristics and part of its behavior. The same thing happens with people, where clearly this is much more evident. While we may think of ourselves as objects in a broad sense, we always observe a part of our own reality. Imagine that you are an object and try to define **all your** characteristics and your behavior, that is, all the attributes that you can find, starting perhaps with your eye color, height, weight, size of your ears, even those that cannot be observed, such as your document number, academic background, diseases you had, and countless others. When we talk about behavior, try to include everything you know how to do, right or wrong. From talking to solving crossword puzzles. Surely if you do the whole exercise, it will be endless.

Consequently, when we observe an object, we are only interested in one part, the one that is relevant to the problem we want to solve, therefore, we make an abstraction of the object, filtering out everything that does not interest us. Therefore, although the object may exist physically, what we are really interested in is a part, an abstraction that we ourselves build.

If we think about the object "student" that, although is a person, perhaps we are interested in some attributes like his address, document number, career, exam grades and a few others. And the actions that a student can perform within this context may be, perhaps, register in careers, in subjects, take exams, apply for certain certificates, make certain formalities. While we cannot deny that the student is a person, we are not interested in knowing absolutely everything, only what is necessary for the issue we want to model in order to solve a problem. In this sense, it does not matter his eye color or weight, nor if he is a good cook or if he makes his bed every morning. These characteristics may be relevant in another context.

Even without thinking about objects derived from such complex realities, we can see that a bank account for the bank system has a certain complexity. The bank will be interested in knowing every movement that was made in the account, as well as an amount of data about its client. However, within another context outside the bank, it may only be relevant to know the account number and the name of the holder. It is the same account, different contexts, different objects.

This is how we now come to the last part of the definition: the "limited reality". Whenever we look for objects within a problem, we do so thinking about that problem, which puts limits on reality. Therefore, objects will always be formed by those parts that are relevant within each problem. Something that seems to us to be one thing can represent different objects in different contexts.

In a broad sense, everyone is an object, we are all objects in some context, and we are not always the same object.

The Object-Oriented Paradigm

The time has come to define what we can understand by "paradigm" and in particular how we associate this word with objects.

The word paradigm represents a typical example or model of something.

It seems simple, but this concept encompasses a set of ideas worth analyzing.

Paradigms are useful, because they say a lot with little. They include many ideas that we can even deal with prejudices, in the good sense of the word, about something. For example, if we say that a person is a paradigm of order, we can imagine a series of characteristics of that person, even without having observed them. We could think that his room is tidy, that it is easy for him to find his things, that he keeps a careful agenda and even that he is punctual for his appointments. If we say that a country represents the paradigm of modernity, we can imagine many things too, without having visited it. For example, we can almost assure that it will have good public services, that the bureaucracy will be highly efficient, that we will find technology to the service of the citizen.

All of these assumptions, and more, will come to us only from a brief statement.

The use of paradigms provides us, then, with great power of synthesis. Applied in other contexts, if I ask you to build a chair, you will surely appeal, without realizing it, to the part of the definition of "paradigm" where it talks about models. Without thinking about any particular chair, you will know that it should have something like legs, a place to sit and another place to rest your back. Just saying chair, says a lot of things.

And what does this have to do with programming? Well, it turns out that we can classify languages according to their adherence to different paradigms, or sets of ideas that determine their essential characteristics. Perhaps you have already used some structured programming language. In them we can find procedures, functions, understand the concept of effective modularity, other concepts such as functional independence, cohesion, coupling, and we also know that to solve a problem we must decompose it into sub-problems that are likely to become one or more sub-programs. All this, just by saying that a language is structured.

On the other hand, if we are in front of another language and we are told that it adheres to the functional programming paradigm, we will know what we can expect from it. Surely we will have to interpret the problem through a set of functions, functions composed of other functions, and we will only have to study how these ideas are implemented in that language.

This has an amazing power, because by knowing the ideas behind each paradigm, we can know a lot about language without even studying it in depth.

For more than four decades, object-oriented programming has grown enormously in popularity. The time has come, then, to identify those ideas behind such a popular and powerful paradigm, and we will try to decipher the reason for its success.

For the object oriented programming paradigm, a problem is composed, and is solved from a set of objects that collaborate with each other.

This idea is not only simple but, at least for me, it is absolutely natural.

When we observe a problem in reality, we can present ourselves before at least three alternatives: ask ourselves under a structured look, what procedures and functions we can find, inquire about which functions and composition of functions are present, or, thirdly, try to identify which objects participate in that problem.

I'll definitely take the last one. I assume that there are more people who go through life observing objects than those who see sub-programs or functions while performing their daily activities. As simple as looking out the window and describing what we observe.

The main foundation of the object paradigm is that it represents a way of thinking that is more natural to us. For this reason, it is surely that its diffusion increases with respect to other paradigms. Surely that's where we should look for the reason of its success and its proliferation in so many languages and methodologies.

In the history of some languages we see this journey. For example, the C language was born as an imperative and structured language. Then it evolves toward C++ where it incorporates concepts of the programming oriented to objects.

I also want to clarify that what I have seen in these years is the "transformation" of many languages, which end up being in some sense hybrid, or multi-paradigm.

My intention in this book is to show the theory of objects in the most essential way, from its foundations. The objective is that by understanding as best as possible the ideas on which the object paradigm is based, you can imagine those things that a programming language that adheres to the paradigm should contain.

Another objective is to show, at a basic level, how we can imagine a solution to a problem using objects. There are formal methodologies that allow us to build models and document them. These methodologies are based on what we can observe. Here I intend to show you how we should observe a problem in order to eventually apply those methodologies.

In other words, to solve a problem you must first understand it. If we do not understand it, there will be no methodology that will lead us to a good result. We will see how to understand it, simply by thinking about objects.

What's inside the object paradigm?

In this section, we will see the few concepts that are within this paradigm. Understanding them we will know the main characteristics of the object oriented languages.

Almost by accident, during this tour we will see how we can observe reality by thinking about objects and thus build models of solutions to some problems. Without the need to go into methodological details, in an intuitive way, we will build some models that will allow us to solve problems thinking about objects.

The repetition of the words "thinking about objects" is absolutely intentional. More than anything, when we come from other paradigms, we have to open our minds, unlearn the way we see reality, and accommodate the idea that everywhere there are objects interacting with each other. In this way, everything will be simpler.

Next we will see the essential concepts that we must know, by way of definitions and small examples, that illustrate the ideas.

Object

This looks like déjà vu, but it's not. A few pages ago, I was forced to define the concept of object in a simple, almost superficial way. I had to do so in order to describe the paradigm that is based on them.

To avoid going back a few pages, I will transcribe the definition here.

"An object is any observable entity that has physical or imaginary existence, that has a set of relevant attributes or characteristics, and has a certain behavior within a limited reality."

At this point we are able to describe in more detail what objects are made of, in an ideal sense, and to do this we will start with an example.

Suppose a bank offers its customers two types of accounts. Here I will describe the observable reality of this particular bank. You may know of others with different characteristics, but as a simplified example, this particular reality will be as described below. So, the bank offers the typical savings and checking accounts. A savings account is used, for example, to deposit money and use it through a card, with which you can make purchases using the money deposited. This money will generate interest that will be paid monthly. Besides, other operations can be made, such as withdrawals, transfers, automatic debits, and consultations, both of balances and of last movements. Checking accounts, however, have the possibility of using money that is not available in the account, and for the use of which we will be charged interest, as a loan. On the other hand, it will not pay us interest on the money deposited. In addition, checks may be issued to third parties. Deposits, withdrawals, inquiries and transfers are also permitted. Both types of accounts have your data: account number, holder data as a document, name and address. Checking accounts also need data on your credit profile, in order to give you in agreement an amount of money that you can use without having it. Also each account will store a balance and data on the movements made during its entire existence.

So far the description of reality. Clearly we can distinguish two types of objects: savings and checking accounts. The most astute will also be able to observe that there is, at least, one client and one bank, but we will talk about this later. For now let's concentrate on accounts.

Clearly each object has a set of data and actions associated with it.

From the example given, for now we focus the analysis on the savings accounts. We can observe that it has as data a balance, a client, movements, and in it you can make actions such as deposit, extract, buy, transfer and consult.

We will call the data "attributes", and the actions we will say will be implemented through "methods".

Each attribute of an object will then be another object, containing relevant information, within the context of the problem to be solved.

Each method of an object will consist of instructions written in some object-oriented language that perform the desired action.

For an object to perform a task it must execute one of its methods. This is only possible, if the object receives a "message".

In short, an object has attributes and methods. Attributes define the characteristics that the object has that are relevant within the problem, and methods define all those actions that the object is allowed to perform within the same context. The only way to make an object do something is by sending a message that will trigger the execution of a method.

Suppose we have a savings account, which we will call A. On it we want to make a withdrawal of money of an amount X of pesos. To perform this task we can write something similar to this:

A extract X.

This is just a message that we will interpret as follows: the object A, receives the message "extract" with the argument X. Since A is a "savings account" object, it must have an "extract" method implemented. Within that method things can happen such as determining if the value of X is less than or equal to the balance (which is one of the attributes of the object A). If so, the balance will be extracted and updated. Otherwise, it must be reported that the operation can not be performed.

In summary, it turns out that the objects have several elements associated with them, some of which have already been presented, but not formally, and others that I will present below.

Attribute

An attribute is a quality of an object, which is relevant to the problem we want to solve.

Method

A method is an action performed by an object. It is the algorithmic part of the object.

Message

A message is the way an object can perform an action. A message activates a method, if it is recognized. Otherwise the object will do nothing, or warn that it cannot do such a thing. We can also say that it is the way objects interact with each other.

Encapsulation

An object is like an opaque capsule that holds its attributes and methods and prevents others from modifying its content. It can only be done through its public interface, which is determined by those messages it is capable of responding to.

Information hiding

It is a concept related to the previous one. Attributes are private to the object, and are hidden from the outside of it. They can only be accessed from inside the object. To assign a value to an attribute or modify it, it can only be done through a method that is defined within it. Therefore, I can only access them through sending messages, if there are methods that allow it.

Class

Another concept of object theory that we must define is "class".

When we observe reality, we perceive a set of individual objects. For example, if we enter a university we can observe students, teachers, and other people doing different activities. Although we see individual objects, under certain circumstances we can interpret that many of them have something in common. We can also imagine things that are not seen, such as the fact that each student belongs to at least one career, and that in that career there are several subjects, and within that environment things happen, many things. The students take exams, the professors are part of courts, some finish their careers and get a degree, others have lunch at the university canteen, some get scholarships, others play cards in some free time. All this simply by observing actions, if we think about attributes, the amount can be infinite.

This tells us that reality is very complex, but fortunately we do not need to model everything that happens. We must concentrate only on the problem to be solved. Then we apply a "filter" and observe only what is relevant to our objective.

If the problem involves the need to record the academic status of each student, and the actions that each one of them takes within that scope, the teachers immediately disappear from the scene. So do the university canteen and the card game, among other things. We will only focus on the students, who will have an identification, a name, a record of the careers in which they are enrolled, the subjects they are studying, the exams, which they took, and the actions they can perform, such as enrolling in careers, dropping out, taking exams, and perhaps a few other things. In this way, reality becomes simpler, and we can see in this context that all students are "equal". In what sense? In the sense that all of them are interested in knowing the same things and they can perform only a few actions, within the context of the problem to be modeled.

In this way we see that, although there are many "student" objects, in a way they are all the same. They have the same characteristics or attributes, and are capable of performing the same actions. They only differ from each other in their identity, and in the values that their attributes can take.

The "student" objects, then, are similar, and within that resemblance they have between them, only the values of their attributes can vary, but the quantity and semantics of them should never vary, nor the actions that each similar object can perform.

Digression: Let's suppose the strange situation in which there are two identical twins, who are called the same by the mischief of their parents, and who by mistake were assigned the same ID card, who are in the same career, take the same subjects and get the same grades. Are they both the same object? We can say that they are two equal objects, but not identical. Two different objects always differ in their identity. It is not the same being as being identical. To be identical, for the theory of objects, means only that we refer to the same object.

We conclude then, that the objects that we consider similar, belong to the same "class", consequently, we are already able to propose a definition:

A class is a generic specification of an arbitrary number of similar objects.

By saying that it is the "generic specification", we are affirming that the class contains all the characteristics that define the objects created from it. We also say that it specifies an arbitrary number of objects, because the number of objects I need from that class within a problem is anyone. From zero to a huge number.

I know you're wondering how a class can exist without objects. Well, it's very simple. If we are modeling the student registration system of a new university, there will be the student class, from which we can create the "student" objects, but until the first one arrives and registers, there will be that class and no objects.

There is a misconception that a class is a set of similar objects. While the idea is attractive it is absolutely false. It is not true, from any point of view, that a class is a set of objects. The class is something like the "factory" of objects. If we have a car factory, it is nothing more than a mechanism that allows us to create instances of the "car" object. It does not mean that the factory is a set of cars. Another example that I once read and found interesting is that of cookie production. Let's suppose we are going to make cookies, prepare the dough and spread it. We're ready to cut it, in the shape that the cookies will have. For that we can use those cookie cutters that have some shape. They're usually made of some kind of metal, and they can be shaped like a little heart, a little rabbit, or just circles. That element contains the generic specification of the shape of an arbitrary number of cookies, but in no way can we say that it's a set of cookies. If it were, the cookie cutter would be edible, and clearly it is not.

At this point we are clear about what a class is, and what it is not.

We are now in a position to call a spade a spade. In the example of the bank accounts, we saw the example of withdrawing a sum of money, by sending a message. That message was

A extract X.

Now, using the correct terminology, we can say that the object A, which is of the class "savings account", receives the message extract, with the argument X, which most likely will belong to some numerical class.

Instance

Apparently, a class then appears as a factory of objects. And that's pretty accurate. Consequently, we can ask ourselves: How are objects born?

The answer to this question is: instantiation.

Creating an instance, or instantiating, is the process by which we send a message to a class to create a new object, based on its specifications.

Consequently, object belonging to a class, and instance of a class are synonymous. Object and instance are the same.

Every time I need an object from a class, I have to instantiate it.

Putting it all together: Objects, classes and messages

Let's put it all together through a simple example.

Let's suppose that within a problem we need rectangles. We have as data its base and height, and we need to know its perimeter and area.

At first sight, we can infer that the attributes of the triangle object are base and height, and we need the perimeter and area methods to be able to solve the problem.

In principle, we can say that the class that allows us to create the rectangles of our problem could look like this:

Rectangle
base (real) height (real)
perimeter area

The upper block defines the class name, the middle block its attributes and the lower block its methods. We can indicate, as shown, that we expect that both the attribute "base" and the attribute "height", belong to the class of real numbers. The methods "perimeter" and "area" do not have arguments, because they do not need them.

The "perimeter" method could be written more or less like this:

perimeter
 ^ (base+height)*2.

What is this notation? It is a notation based on the syntax of the Smalltalk language, which is one of the best interpretations of the object paradigm. The ^ symbol represents the action of returning a result, and what follows is a known arithmetic expression, which uses the attributes of the object. As the method is executed within a given instance, these attributes are accessed from the method without any problem. Finally, the dot indicates that the message is finished. Yes, I wrote message and not instruction, because every method, when written, results in a succession of messages.

Following the same reasoning, the area method would look like this:

area
 ^ (base*height).

Is this correct? In principle it seems so, except for one detail. Since the attributes of an object are inaccessible from outside of itself, we need methods to assign values to them. We can write a method to assign a value to each attribute, or a unique method, which we will call "construct", that assigns values to both. In this way, the triangle class would be as follows:

Rectangle
base (real) height (real)
construct (b,h) perimeter surface

It would only remain to define the new method "construct", which has two arguments that we call a and h. We do not need to define what kind of arguments are.

construct (b,h)
   base:=b.
   height:=h.

If we want to know the perimeter and the area of a rectangle with base 8 and height 3, we should create an instance, assign the values to its attributes and obtain the results, in the following way:

A:=New rectangle.
A construct (8,3).
A perimeter.
A area.

The first is a message sent to the class Rectangle, indicating that we want a new instance, and the object A, receives the assignment method with that instance as an argument.

The second message is sent to object A, which is already a new rectangle. The message is construct, with the arguments 8 and 3 that will be assigned to base and height respectively.

The third message will return the perimeter value, which in this case is 22.

The fourth message will return the value of the area, which in this case is 24.

Abstraction

The process of abstraction consists of separating what we consider relevant, conceptually isolating what is not. Clearly when we think about the objects of a problem we apply a process of abstraction.

When talking about objects, I suggested that you try to list all your characteristics and all the actions you are capable of performing. Obviously this is an impossible task to do. However, if now I propose that you do it only in one area of all that you perform, surely you could do it.

In fact, when we think of a university student, within the context of the university system, the characteristics and actions that are relevant are quite limited.

That's an abstraction. We separate what is relevant from what is not.

That same student is also a person who has other properties and performs other tasks, for example, as a customer of the cell phone company. There, it is not relevant what career he is studying, or what grade he got in math, nor is it relevant for the university if the student has any debt with the cell phone company.

One person, multiple realities, multiple abstractions, multiple objects.

When we observe a problem, we **must find** objects. We observe objects, but immediately, once we obtain them, we must classify, that is, we must design the classes that are capable of creating them. There is the first step of the process of abstraction.

Then there is one more process of abstraction, and we can apply it once we have all the classes of the problem accurately determined.

We will apply the concept of abstraction to the classes we know we need.

Let's see this with an example, and then put names to things.

Let's take the example of the bank that we had abandoned and incomplete. There we said that we had two types of accounts, a savings account and a checking account.

We can design the classes that instantiate these objects, for example, in the following simplified way:

Savings Account
construct ( )   deposit ( )   extract ( )   transfer ( )   seeBalance   seeMovements   closeAccount   calculateInterest

In this class we can see that the owner is a customer, which will be another class that we should model, but is not relevant at this time. There will also be a class of operations, which we will not model, but we know that an attribute of the savings account is the set or list of operations that have been made throughout the life of the account. On the other hand, by way of simplification, the methods with attributes were indicated only with the use of parentheses.

In the same way, we can model the "Checking Account" class, more or less like this:

Checking Account
account number   owner (customer)   balance   movements (list of operations)   InterestRateCollect   discoveredAuthorized   checksEmitted (check list)

Checking Account
construct ( )
deposit ( )
extract ( )
transfer ( )
Paycheck ( )
seeSaldo
seeMovements
closeAccount
calculateInterest

We can see that although they are different classes, they have several elements in common, both if we observe the attributes and the methods.

Applying another process of abstraction, we will separate those things that we consider equal or common, and we will create a new class Account.

Account
account number owner (customer) balance movements (list of operations)
deposit ( ) seeSaldo seeMovements

It looks like that's it. However, you may wonder why there are no methods to construct, extract(), transfer(), closeAccount and calculateInterests. What will be the answer? The idea was to separate that which is common, which is the same in both classes. These methods have the same name, but they are not equal. Building these different classes is certainly a process that requires some analysis, because both account classes do not have the same attributes. Withdrawing money is not the same in both classes, because in the current account the money available is the sum of the balance plus the authorized overdraft, and in the savings account you can withdraw only an amount that is less than or equal to the balance. On the other hand, the savings account pays interest and the checking account charges interest. These are clearly different methods, so they are not eligible in this abstraction process.

Now the class model would look like this:

Account

account number
owner (customer)
balance
movements (list of operations)

deposit ( )
seeSaldo
seeMovements

Savings Account

interest ratePay

construct ( )
extract ( )
transfer ( )
closeAccount
calculateInterest

Checking Account

InterestRateCollect
discoveredAuthorized
checksEmitted (check list)

construct ( )
extract ( )
transfer ( )
Paycheck ( )
closeAccount
calculateInterest

Analyzing the problem, looking at reality, we had found two kinds of accounts, and now we have three. What happened? Is this right?

The correct answer would be: it depends. And it depends on what we do with the new class we just created.

Now we are ready to apply the concept of abstraction again. When creating the class "Account" we put a filter on "Savings Account" and "Checking Account", so that we can model what is common to both, creating an interesting class, but incomplete in some sense.

The interesting thing is that, if we made the union between each of the two resulting classes with the class "Account", we would get the original classes. And this union occurs, in the theory of objects, through the mechanism of **inheritance.**

In order to observe this mechanism, we can draw the three classes obtained with a hierarchical distribution.

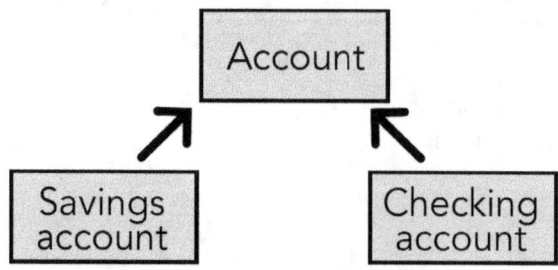

We see that the Account class is above Savings Account and Checking Account. That fact causes the lower classes to "inherit" the attributes and methods of the higher class. Which ones? All of them!

The Account class is rated Super Class for the other two. On the contrary, Savings Account and Checking Account are Sub-Classes of the Account class.

What happened was that by applying a process of abstraction we created a class that did not exist before, precisely because it is not part of the reality we want to model. That's why it's called an Abstract Class.

In the middle of this story, two new concepts appeared that deserve to be defined: Inheritance and Abstract Class. That is why we will dedicate some paragraphs to them so that they will be perfectly clear.

Inheritance

Trough the inheritance we can create new classes from another one, containing all the definitions that this one has, being able to add or to redefine some of them.

"Inheritance is the mechanism by which one class is created as a superset of another.

Seen in this way, the Savings Account class, contains all the Account definitions (its attributes and methods), and adds others. Therefore, it is a super-set.

It may happen that in a sub-class you need to redefine some method. In that case, I only have to create it with the same name as it has in the superclass, and the content (the method code made of messages), modified according to the needs.

To give an example of this last idea, let's suppose we have N classes that have several elements in common, then we create an abstract class, or super class of these Ns, that contains all these characteristics that are common. Now let us also suppose that in only one of these Ns there is a method that is implemented in a different way. In that case, even though it is defined in the superclass, we redefine it with the same name in the subclass where this method is different, and it will be the one that will act for its instances.

In the case of bank accounts the "deposit" method is identical in both, therefore we have decided to define it in the super-class "Account". Now let's suppose that we create a new type of account. The bank came up with the idea of creating an account that doubles the amount of the deposits (this is an assumption, that will never happen). Then there is a difference between depositing into that new account class, consequently, we add to the newly created sub-class a "deposit" method, which includes this special feature, redefining then the super-class method, only for this new class.

The fundamental advantage of the inheritance mechanism is that it allows the written code to be reused. If several classes share functionalities, we only have to implement them once in the super-class, saving us from writing and maintaining duplicate, triplicate or multiplied code.

Abstract Class

It became clear that the abstract class "Account", emerged as a design decision that allows to take advantage of the mechanism of inheritance.

We rightly call it "abstract" because it results from an intellectual process of abstraction applied to defined classes, and not from the perception of real objects. They exist on a higher level of abstraction.

Let's clarify this with an example. Suppose I arrive at the bank, sit down in front of the appropriate employee, Tom for the example, and say "good morning Tom, I'm here to open a new account". What will Tom say to me? He will probably ask me, "Do you want to open a savings or checking account? What happened? I simply went with a request that was outside of his reality, positioning myself on a higher level of abstraction. Tom needed more precision to be able to relate my claims to the objects he knows. So he "lowered" me to his level of abstraction, where the real objects he knew existed, offering me the possibility of creating an object that the bank actually handled.

Let's take abstraction to another level. To do this let's think about nature, and the processes of abstraction. Suppose that Mary and John each have a pet. Mary has a dog and John has a cat. The dog is a poodle called X, and the cat is a Siamese called Y. Both are observable objects of reality. Now we can get our creative brain going, and think that X is a dog, and has things in common with others, so we can imagine a class Dog. We can also observe that Y is a cat, and has things in common with others, so we can imagine a class Cat. We observed that there are other animals that share some things in common with Dog, such as wolves, and we decided to create a Canid class. We also see things in common between Cat and other animals like tigers and leopards, and decided to create a Feline class. These are abstract classes, because they arise from our own process of abstraction, and do not exist in reality. We go further. Canids with Felines have things in common with Camelids and other species, forming the super-class Vertebrate, which together with Invertebrates can form the super-class Animal. In turn, between the Animal class and others, like the one derived from plants, we can create a superior super-class called Living Beings.

Within this great hierarchy, some are sub-classes of others and at the same time super-classes of some. Consequently, these terms are relative to their location.

Now, if we want to instantiate a horse, a dog, a cat or a canary, we have no problem. We can imagine that. Now if we go up to the level of abstraction everything can get complicated. Let's try to instantiate the Feline class. But it's not a cat or a tiger, but a feline in general. There is no such thing. Much less if we want to instantiate a vertebrate. Details are missing, the level of abstraction is too high to be able to imagine its instances. Therefore, in most cases, it does not make sense to instantiate the abstract classes, simply because they do not create any object that is within the reality we are modeling.

If we continue to climb the pyramid of abstraction, at the last level, at the top, we will find the most abstract class of all, from which all the others derive. That will be the "Object" class.

This means that all the classes that we create to model the reality of a given problem will fall within a class hierarchy. In the most common case, the classes we get will depend on the "Object" class.

For example, in Smalltalk language this class is called Object, and has among other subclasses Magnitude, on which depend, for example, all the numbers of different classes.

Class Hierarchy

Being intentionally repetitive once again, we can then conclude that all classes are part of a large hierarchical structure, that they use the mechanism of inheritance to reuse everything defined in the classes that are hierarchically above them.

The hierarchical structure helps to order both existing classes and new classes that we need to create. I invite you to think what would happen if this structure did not exist.

The use of written code has not only to do with inheritance, but, over time, it is very likely that we have created classes that at some point served to solve one problem, and later will serve to solve others. The class hierarchy is growing, it is enriched by everything we create. It is as if we were learning in some way, and over the years we will have a library of classes enriched with all our work, and in a collaborative way, with the work of others who wish to share, being able to access a universal library of classes that solve classic problems.

How do you run a method?

When an object receives a message, it looks for a method with that name within its class. If it doesn't find it, it looks for it in its superclass, and so on until it finds it. In that case it executes it. Otherwise, it might give an error message that the object cannot respond to the message.

Now we can understand why a method can be redefined. A few pages ago we saw an example of a method that existed in a class and in its super-class. Which one will be executed when a message is received? Clearly the search is done from bottom to top within the class hierarchy, so it will always run the first one found, following that search order.

Polymorphism

Many times, objects of different kinds will need to respond to the same message.

Let us suppose that in the animal kingdom everyone can understand the message "drink water". Somehow everyone does, but we can differentiate the procedure that each of them follows. Usually we do it using a glass. A dog will use its tongue, something similar to what a cat will do, since both can make their tongue look like a spoon. A cow, however, cannot do that and does it by sipping. An elephant uses its trunk. The message could be as follows:

X takeWater.

X being any animal. The message is the same, but the method that each one uses is different and depends on the class that X belongs to.

Let's analyze the following expression:

A + B.

Most of us would think that there are two numerical variables that add up. Something very simple. Where is the polymorphism? Precisely in the classes to which A and B belong. To be strict with the theory of objects, there is no arithmetic expression there, there is a message. It should be read as follows: The object A receives the message + with the argument B. If A and B turn out to be numbers, it is all very clear. It happens that this expression, or message, which can be inside a program, at the time of writing does not know the class to which the objects will belong and will try to respond to that message anyway when the time comes. If A and B were integers, he will add them, if they were arrays and the class arrays defined with that operation exists, he will also do it. If they were strings of characters perhaps it will concatenate the content of A and B, if they were rabbits and they had implemented the + method because it will add them as it has been defined.

We can define polymorphism as follows:

Polymorphism is the ability of two or more objects of different classes to respond appropriately to the same message.

Without a doubt, the polymorphism facilitates programming. Using previous examples, it could be that inside the program that executes an ATM the following message appears:

X extract Y.

Account X gets the message "extract" with the argument Y. Whether X is a savings account or a checking account, the message will be answered by executing the corresponding method. Then we write the message once and it works every time. Even if we add a new type of account, we will not have to modify this expression, because there will surely be a way to respond appropriately to such a message.

If we were facing a conventional language, we should fill in the "if" code, asking what kind of account is to execute the proper procedure. Here that does not happen.

Dynamic Linking

Dynamic binding refers to the ability of certain programming languages to define the data type of their variables at runtime.

Note that the terms "variables" and "data types" were used, that is, it is a characteristic of some programming languages, regardless of the paradigm they adhere to.

If we accommodate the phrase to the object paradigm, we should say that dynamic linking refers to the ability of any object-oriented language to establish the class of the objects that act as variables at runtime.

It is basically the same, just the terminology changes so, if we talk about object oriented languages, all of them without exception must have dynamic linking.

Why is this so? There is a relationship between polymorphism and dynamic linking. Although both characteristics can exist independently, polymorphism makes true sense because of the existence of the dynamic linking. In a strongly typed language, the expression C:=A+B is always going to mean the same thing, since the variables A, B and C already have a data type assigned at code time, so they will always be executed in the same way.

On the other hand, in an object-oriented language, the same expression C:=A+B will have different behaviors, depending on the classes of the objects A, B and C. And this can only happen thanks to the dynamic linking, which makes that at the moment of the execution the classes of the objects can vary according to what has happened before.

Based on an example already known, if we are in an ATM and we want to extract X dollars, we insert the card, select which account we want to make the extraction from, and then possibly execute the message C extract X. Depending on the class chosen for C, the corresponding method will be executed, applying the polymorphism.

In short, what we should expect from an object-oriented language, is that the variables that it should use, which are definitely objects, can adopt any class within the program execution, therefore, it is not possible to determine its class permanently.

A universe of objects

If we say that we are surrounded by objects, we are not wrong. In the object-oriented paradigm, all are objects that contain other objects, up to a reasonable level. For example, we can imagine a person, which is an object that has, for example, an address. That address is an object, which has other attributes such as country, province, city, neighborhood, street, number, floor, department. Street can also be an object that has a name, orientation, and for a GPS it can have a succession of points that determine its layout in the map through geographical coordinates.

Even in an object-oriented language, familiar control structures such as decisions and cycles are only objects that decide and iterate. We'll see examples of this later.

Everything is translated into a universe of objects and messages.

How to solve problems by thinking about objects

Apparently, getting involved within this paradigm forces us to think differently. Much more if we come of programming in other paradigms.

When we are faced with this paradigm we are forced to think about objects. When we face a new problem, we must visualize the objects that participate there, interacting and collaborating among them, through the forms of communication that we already know, that is, through sending messages between them.

Let us suppose that we have a narrative that describes a problem that we must solve. Without pretending to develop a formal methodology, I am going to propose a kind of grammatical analysis of the narrative that can help us identify these objects.

First we can identify the nouns. Each one we find is a candidate to become an object. On the other hand, we will identify adjectives, which describe qualities of the objects, and verbs, which indicate actions to be performed.

In a normal sentence, we find a subject and a predicate. It is very likely that the subject is an object and the predicate is a method.

Let's look at a simple example:

The dog barks.

It is clear that the object is the dog and the action of barking is nothing more than a method that will be executed when the appropriate message is received.

Let's look at a slightly more complex example.

The client withdraws $100 from his savings account.

There we find the objects "client" and "savings account". In this case, the savings account in the sentence acts as a direct object. Then, thinking as the object paradigm indicates, the "client" object sends the message "extract $100" to the "savings account" object. Then, in this way the method is implemented within this last object "savings account", being "client" the object that sends the message. So, we can perceive the collaborative communication that exists between the objects of the problem.

Adjectives most of the times, will be attributes of some objects.

The result of identifying the objects will be to design classes that are capable of instantiating them. Here it may happen that some objects are also attributes of others. This is normal, and frequent. For example, in the phrase "every customer must inform his address", we identify two objects: "customer" and "address". Address is an object in itself, and is a composite object as we saw earlier. However, it is also an attribute of the object "customer".

To illustrate these ideas, we will look at some examples that will allow us to see how we can solve problems by thinking about objects. As we go deeper into problem solving, new kinds of interesting objects will appear, and different ways of dealing with them through their methods. If it were necessary to write some portion of methods or programs, I will continue using a generic pseudocode, but very similar to the Smalltalk language.

The family tree

A family tree is a representation of a set of people related through ties of descent and ancestry.

Within a family tree, and taking a particular person as a reference, we will be able to see who their parents, uncles, grandparents, children, nephews, cousins, and a long etcetera are, if the tree is leafy and complete.

Let's think about how many classes we need to represent the objects we find within a family tree. Could it be that we need different classes for each relationship? I don't think so, since kinships are relative to the person I take as a reference. Person X can have Y as his father, but for Y person X is his son. Z, the father of Y will be the grandfather of X. He is both a father and a grandfather, and he may also be someone's son. So there is no such thing as kinship.

On second thought, there are only persons.

Now, what attributes do these persons have?

Basically, a person will have data to identify him. In a family tree, not much information is needed. Just the name, date of birth, place perhaps, and not much else. The most important information for the tree to be constructed is, for each person, who their parents are.

Then we will have a class Person, with two essential attributes, which we will call "father" and "mother".

Now, what kind will these attributes be? What information is relevant from the parents to build the family tree? We might think that the name is enough, but it would be ambiguous and incomplete. Ambiguous because perhaps several people have the same name.

The best way to identify the objects "father" and "mother" turns out to be that these attributes are of the class "Person".

Somehow, we will build a recursive class, since two of its attributes are of the same class we are building.

This is basically possible because in most object-oriented languages, attributes or variables are actually pointers to objects.

Thus, the class up to now would look like this:

Person
name
date of birth
placeBirth
parent (Person)
mother (Person)
construct()
...other methods

Within the construct method, beyond determining the values for name, dateBirth and placeBirth, the objects to be assigned to parent should preferably already exist.

It is obvious that the first person we instantiate will not have these attributes, since we have no other people on the family tree. It would be impossible to make a family tree complete, since it would have to contain all of humanity from its origins, and yet, if such a thing were possible, we would have at least two people without their defined parents. Consequently, we will accept that some people will not have their parents defined, but we will obviate their consequences in order to simplify the problem.

Let's build some simple methods. For example, we basically need a method to ask a person's name.

The message could be as follows:

X seeName.

And the implementation in pseudocode will be something like that:

seeName
^ name.

As X is the object that receives the message, and the method is executed inside it, we have access to its attributes, then through the ^ operator we show the name.

We will also need methods witch, given an object "Person", make known who his father is and who his mother is.

The messages could be:

X seeFather.
X seeMother.

And its implementation:

seeFather
^ father.

seeMother
^ mother.

Now, if we want to ask a person what their name is, I can do so:

X seeName.

And if you would like to ask her what her mother's name is:

X seeMother seeName.

This is because the message will be executed from left to right. First the object X receives the seeMother message, the result is an object of the class "Person" that turns out to be the mother of X. To this partial result we send then the seeName message, so we will see the "name" attribute of the "mother" object of X.

Let's start creating interesting methods. Now suppose we want to determine if two people are siblings (just to simplify sexual orientation issues), and for that we will define that it happens if they have the same mother or father.

To solve this query, we need two objects, two persons. One receives a message with another person as an argument, and we can represent it like this:

X isSiblingOf: Y.

Clearly the object X receives the message isBrotherFrom, with the argument Y. Both X and Y must be objects already created and of the class "Person".

Let's try to write the method isSiblingOf. The result should simply be a true or false, so we will show the result of a logical expression.

isSiblingOf: a
^ (father == a seeFather) or (mother == a seeMother).

First let us note that, while the pseudocode resembles smalltalk, it is not smalltalk in a strict sense.

The == operator will mean "identical", that is, we are referring to the same object. It is not equivalent to the = operator, since it has been established that equality is not the same as identity.

Consequently, evaluating the logical expression, if the father of the object that receives the message is the same as that of the argument, or the mother of the object that receives the object is the same as that of the argument, then both are siblings.

Everything seems to be fine, except that the following may happen:

X isSiblingOf: X.

This message would give us a true result, which can lead to philosophical discussions. We should ask ourselves, am I my own brother? Clearly the answer should be "false". However, the proposed method does not resolve it correctly. Let us correct that error:

isSiblingOf: a
^ ((father == a seeFather) or (mother == a seeMother)) and (self <> a).

Now it is resolved. Of course, only if we understand what the word "self" does there. The object "self" refers to the one who receives the message. Consequently, in that part of the proposition we evaluate whether the argument object is different from the object that receives the message, thus solving the error of the previous method.

Having already a method to identify siblings, it would be simple to build a method for uncles and aunts. We will use "uncle" as neutral gender for "aunt or uncle". X will be someone's uncle, if he is his father's or mother's sibling, being able to reuse the method isSiblingOf.

Let's call the method isUncleOf, leaving the message as follows:

X isUncleOf: Y.

And its corresponding method will be:

isUncleOf: a
^ (self isSiblingOf: a seeFather) or (self isSiblingOf: a seeMother).

Now, knowing if X is someone's nephew is also much easier, since X is Y's nephew if Y is X's uncle. Once again, we will use nephew as neutral gender for "nephew or niece".

The message would be:

X isNephewOf: Y.

And its corresponding method:

enNephewOf: a
^ (a isUncleOf: self).

You could easily add cousin methods, since X is a cousin of Y if any parent of X is a sibling of any parent of Y, leaving this method to the reader creativity.

The class "Person", until now would remain more or less like this:

Person

name
Date of birth
placeBirth
parent (Person)
mother (Person)

construct()
seeFather
seeMother
isSiblingOf ()
isUncleOf ()
isNephewOf ()
isCousinOf ()

Now, how could we do so that, given a family tree, we could obtain from it, for example, who are X's uncles?

For this we would need an object "Family" that contains all the people.

We would need objects that contain other objects, and these are called collections.

Object collections

There are several ways to collect objects, which most languages provide. However, it is always possible to add new classes to existing ones.

A collection of objects is composed of a group of objects, which can be of different classes, representing an object relevant to the problem.

It may sound strange that a set of heterogeneous objects forms an object, but in reality this is very common. If we make an analogy with nature and the universe we can find countless examples. We said that the theory on which the object paradigm is based on a natural way of thinking. Yes, both of thinking and of observing reality. Going back to the examples, we can say that the solar system is an object, and at the same time it is a "collection" of objects. It has in its interior the planets, the natural satellites, asteroids, several of them, the sun, and how much object we would like to include in the example. Without a doubt they are heterogeneous objects in the sense that we can divide them into different classes, however, they are part of a single object which is the solar system. Something similar happens with an ocean. It has water, fish and plants of various species. It's an object that collects objects of different kinds. We can also see it in man-made constructions, such as a city.

In the case of the family tree, we need an object to contain the family, which is represented by a group of objects, in this particular case, all of the class "Person".

In a broad sense, a collection can be, for example, an ordered set of characters, or "String". A String is composed of a succession of objects of the class "Character". These objects are ordered according to the sequence of characters you have stored.

It is evident how, for the object-oriented paradigm, not only is everything an object, but also each one is most likely constructed from other, smaller objects.

As stated at the beginning of this book, the objective is to understand the concepts and elements that we find in the paradigm of objects and, therefore, in the languages that adopt it. The essential thing is to know what you will be able to find in order to know how to search specifically for what you need.

Arrangements of objects

There are other types of collections that are a little more complex, such as vectors, or "Array". You may have already used these types of data structures in other, non-object oriented languages.

An array is nothing more than an ordered collection of objects identified by a name and an index. The particularity of these vectors is that each object can be of a different class.

In structured, or strongly typed, languages, an array is built with elements of a certain type. In the object paradigm an array is, in reality, a succession of pointers to objects of any class.

Even one element of an array could perfectly be another array. This would allow us to easily build arrays, or two-dimensional arrays. An array, in short, is nothing more than a vector of vectors of the same size.

The polymophic character of the array elements is interesting. So interesting that it is difficult to find practical examples where they are really useful. This limitation is fundamentally due to our lack of initial training. We must learn to think about objects, and once we do, everything will come up more naturally.

If we think about the example of bank accounts, we could, for example, place them all in an array, whether they are savings accounts or checking accounts, and at the end of the month run the "collectMaintenance" method, which we did not add but which surely exists. They will most likely be different in both classes, either by value or by whatever. We could then go through the entire vector of accounts, applying the same method to each of its objects, regardless of the class to which they belong.

For example, we are going to create a vector called "accs" that contains two objects "a" and "b", being these a savings account and a cheking account respectively.

```
accs := Array new: 2.
accs at: 1 put: a.
accs at: 2 put: b.
```

The first message instances an array of size 2 and assigns it to the object "accs". In the second message the message at:put: is sent to the object "accs", causing the position 1 of the array to point to the object "a". In the third message, a pointer is created from element 2 of the array to object "b".

Now, we came this far because we need an object that can contain all the people in a family tree. We could well create a vector, and place one by one each person inside the vector, with which we could create a "FamilyTree" class, as a vector of people.

While this sounds reasonable, there is one thing that is not entirely convincing. Each person would have an associated sub-index, which is absolutely useless, since in a family it is difficult to find an order. Many times we use vectors because "there is no other choice". We will see if this is the case.

Fortunately, there are other ways to collect objects.

Dictionaries

Continuing with the ordered collections, there are "Dictionaries", both in Smalltalk and in Python and other object-oriented languages. It is a class similar to vectors, where the index instead of being a number is any other object. It can be a word, or even a number as in the case of vectors, but without the restriction of being strictly correlative. Then we could build a Dictionary of people, identified by their document number.

For example, we could have the object "tree", and the persons "a" and "b".

```
tree := Dictionary new.
tree at: 54656 put: a.
tree at: 49384 put: b.
```

That way you could add as many people as you want, knowing their document number. When creating a Dictionary, unlike an Array, it is not necessary to specify the size. Although these details may vary from language to language. The difficulty a dictionary built this way would have in representing a family is that you would have to know everyone's document number. You could also use each person's name as an index, but there could be people with the same name, and that would make it impossible to use.

Bags

Another way to collect objects is by using object bags. Here we will introduce the subclasses of disordered collections. Logically, in a bag you cannot determine any order in the objects, any amount of objects, of different classes can be contained in a bag, even some objects can be more than once into the bag.

Can we have a savings and checking account bag? Yes, we can. As long as we are careful not to put the same account twice into the bag.

Can we have a bag of people belonging to a family tree? Yes, we can. As long as we are careful not to put the same person twice into de bag.

So far, it would seem more reasonable to use a bag instead of the other ordered collections. But we have that disadvantage of repeated objects, which with some care we can solve.

However, we can use bags for other applications, where it is possible to repeat objects, and the order of the objects is irrelevant.

Let's see this piece of code:

t := 'This is a small program that will help us to test the way I can count the number of times a letter appears into a text".
b := Bag new.
t do: [:c| (c isLetter) ifTrue: [b add: c asLowerCase]].
$a to: $z do: [:c| ^ (b occurrencesOf: c)].

Let's see message by message.

In the first message we assign a text to the object called t.

In the second message we created a new bag, which we called "b".

Then something interesting happens. When you send the "do:" message to object "b", the block that is enclosed in square brackets will be executed for each object into "t". Each character of "t" is passed to "c", "(c isLetter)" returns true if the content of "c" is a letter, and if that happens, its value converted to lowercase is added to "b". This is done with [b add: c asLowerCase].

Finally, for the characters from a to z, the number of times each one appears in the "b" bag is shown.

Although it looks quite similar to Smalltalk, I have taken some syntax licenses to make the solution a little easier, especially in the part where the result is shown. The idea is to highlight the power of using collections, and especially the "do:" message. This is one of the so-called "iterators", which allow you to perform cycles associated with actions for each object within a collection.

There are other iterators, which we will see a little later.

Sets

We can also collect objects by using sets.

A set is exactly what we know by that name, that is, a collection of elements (in this case objects), which are not ordered under any criteria, and which does not contain repeated elements.

It would be something like a bag where the repeated elements do not exist.

Apparently it would be the most appropriate class to contain a family tree, since people are not ordered, they are simply linked through their kinship, and there are no repeated people.

Suppose we have an object of the class person, which can be a variable called "I", which contains my data as a person. We also have a collection, which will be a set, containing my family tree, which is called "family", and will be of the class "Set", that is, a set.

Let's say I want to get a subset of "family" from there that are my cousins. It could be solved more or less like this:

```
cousins := Set new.
cousins := select family: [:p| I isCousinOf: p].
```

The first message defines a "cousins" object of the Set class. Then, using another iterator called "select", that selects the family elements stored in "p" that fulfill the condition of being cousins of "I".

Similarly, you can store savings and current accounts in a set, and select those that meet some condition, or do certain things with them, being objects of different classes, taking advantage of the characteristics of polymorphism.

Here we can see the power of heterogeneous object collections and polymorphism.

We could imagine something like that:

```
Animals of the World do: [:a | a jump.].
```

Each animal, whatever class it was, would jump in its own way, and "a" would take the class of the animal in each iteration.

These are some of the strengths of a paradigm that, when correctly applied, increases productivity enormously.

Applying what we learned

Let's put everything back together using some examples. We will pose problems, identify objects and model the classes that seem appropriate to solve them.

As in all cases, solutions to problems can be varied, so here will get, I hope, acceptable solutions, although I accept that they will not be the only possible ones.

Example 1: Integers from different bases

Suppose we need to operate with binary, octal, and hexadecimal integers. We need to operate with them by performing addition, subtraction, product, and integer division.

All operations, including assigning an object a value, are different.

The objects of the problem are clearly determined. They are binary, octal, and hexadecimal numbers. The operations are also defined. In principle we can think of the following class:

Binary
value
:=   +   -   *   \   seeValue

The classes corresponding to the other bases would look identical, they will only vary in the name and implementation of the methods.

For example, the method we call ":=" is used to put something into "value", you should check that the entered digits are valid for base 2 in case of a binary object, that it is valid for base 8 in case of an octal object, and that it is valid for base 16.

Then, an appropriate method should be created for each operation in each base.

It is not interesting or useful to create a class hierarchy, since in this case there is not much to inherit because the algorithm to operate in each base is different. Perhaps only the seeValue method could be common to all classes.

We can modify the class "Binary" adding two
interesting methods, being in the following
way:

Binary
value
:=   +   -   *   \   toDecimal   fromDecimal   seeValue

The toDecimal method converts a binary
number to a decimal, and the fromDecimal
method performs the reverse operation.

These methods can be added for the classes
"Octal" and "Hexadecimal", and be exploited
through polymorphism.

With these two new methods, the arithmetic
operations could change notably, using the
existing ones that every language has to
operate in base 10.

Consequently, an addition method could be
written like this:

+ x
  ^ fromDecimal(toDecimal value + x verValue toDecimal).

In this way, all arithmetic operations would have the same expression, so they could be inherited from a super-class that we can call "Number".

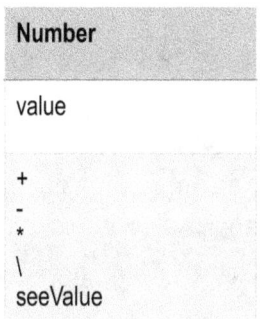

I invite you to create the resulting class hierarchy, to implement some methods.

Example 2: Supermarket receipt

Let's see what objects are inside a supermarket receipt. It is not the intention to model the entire billing system, simply to try to identify the relevant objects that make up a receipt.

Let's assume that they are sales to final consumers, without loyalty programs that identify the customer. In that case, we will simply have the detail of the receipt, with quantity of articles, description, perhaps a code, a unit amount and a subtotal. At the bottom we can find the total to pay and perhaps the payment method used, and eventually the change.

One line could look like this:

```
5 XYX Rice $18.50      $92.50
```

And the foot could be something like that:

```
TOTAL:           $189.45
Cash:            $100.00
Credit Card:     $ 89.45
Change:          $  0.00
```

Clearly we can imagine that we will need a "receipt" object, which will contain the detail and the foot. Within the detail you can see lines, which contain items, that have a price, a quantity, which is an attribute that also depends on the line, and an amount, which depends on the item and the quantity.

An interesting question here is, do price and amount need to be attributes of the line? Well, we can take the price of the item and calculate it on the spot, but this has a drawback. Prices vary over time and the receipt has an unalterable value. It is therefore advisable to copy the values of these attributes to the receipt line. Since the receipt contains several lines, the "body" of the receipt would consist of a collection of lines. Which collection should we choose? I would think that the order is important, in case we need to repeat the printing of the receipt for some reason. Consequently, the body could be represented by an array of lines. At the end, the foot will have the total and a collection of means of payment with their amounts, which should be added up to calculate the change.

Let's see how the classes we need to create these objects would looks like. These classes will have the minimum attributes and methods needed to represent a receipt.

Article
code description price stock
construct() seeDescription see Price

We included the attribute "stock", perhaps the only one that was not mentioned in the problem, since when an item is sold it is very likely that it must be discounted from the existing quantity, and since we modeled the class "Item", we incorporated it.

Line
quantity description priceUnit subtotal
construct(item, quantity) print show

Here we may not include the subtotal, which is calculated by multiplying "unit price" by "quantity". It is only there for the sake of clarity in the explanation, but if it were a real implementation, it probably wouldn't be. Another thing that may attract attention from this class is that it does not make reference to which receipt it belongs to and in what order it should be. If it were a classical relational model, we would have to specify it, but since they are objects, and they have their own identity, they are directly linked to an array inside the receipt, so such references are unnecessary.

PayingInstrument
code description
construct() seeDescription

This class serves to contain the different means of payment instruments accepted.

paymentsOfAReceipt
payingInstrument amount
cosntruct() print show

This class will serve to instantiate the different instruments of payment used within a receipt.

And finally, the most expected class!

Receipt
date time detail(line array) payment(array of paymentsOfAReceipt) total change
construct() addLine addPaymentInstrument printHead printFoot show

For the attributes "total" and "change" applies the same observations we made for the attribute "subtotal" in the class

"Line". While they can be calculated, they are there for the sake of clarity, and perhaps also for efficiency.

The "show" methods will serve to view a receipt without the need to print it, for an eventual consultation. In fact, the receipt is not only printed as it is issued, but also displayed on the screen.

Example 3: The video rental store

This problem is an old acquaintance for those of us who have some years: A video rental store.

This video rental store in particular, turns out to be a place that is dedicated to the rental of films to its members. Some films may be repeated in several copies, in order to satisfy the demand of the members. The working scheme is very simple: each film is rented for 48 hours at a fixed price, except for those considered as premieres, which are rented for 24 hours, and of course have a higher price. Each member can have a maximum of 5 films, and cannot rent more, unless it is a lifetime member, in which case the limit does not exist. If the member does not return the film rented within the stipulated period, the member will be charged a penalty equivalent to twice the amount of the rental for each day of delay. It is also necessary to keep a simple accounting record where the money paid in each day is noted, and at the end a form is issued showing the detail of income.

Well, so far the description of the problem. It may be complete or missing details, which we can ask, or which we should add with good judgment. Be careful about adding "details". In some cases I have seen very imaginative people who add all kinds of elements to a problem, which had nothing to do with reality.

Since this is not a problem-solving book, and a problem can have multiple solutions, we will limit ourselves to consider how we should observe reality, and thus outline an object-based solution.

Let's try to identify objects. By doing a more or less grammatical analysis, we can obtain the following candidate objects:

Video rental store, films, members, copies, releases, life membership, accounting record, income tax return.

There are other elements such as rental price, rental period, maximum amount of movies to be rented, penalty fee, days of delay.

We may also see actions such as renting, returning, issuing income tax returns.

These actions can trigger others. For example, it is not difficult to infer that the devolution of a movie could generate a record of money coming in, eventually a penalty fee, update the number of movies rented by the member, and perhaps other things.

There is another element, which is the rent itself, that we could discuss if it is a candidate object or not. Rent is a verb, but renting itself is not. Renting is an action that generates important data that must be recorded, therefore, it is both, results in an action that generates a relevant object.

Among the objects we find both clients and lifetime customers. The question is, are they two different kinds of objects? Yes and they would not be correct answers. That is, it depends. In principle one could consider that being for life or not is an attribute, which has the only consequence of extending the limit of films that the partner can rent. So it could well be an attribute of the object "member". If we think that in the future we could do different things with the life members, we could now, in a preventive way, and with a semantic sense, think that they are different objects. Something similar happens with ordinary films and premieres. The latter are rented for a different period and have a higher rental price.

Let's try then, to imagine the classes needed to solve the problem.

MEmber: There will be a member class to create partners who will rent the films and pay for them.

Film: Do we really have films? We may need your data, but in a strict sense we don't have movies, and nobody does. Each film has a title, a genre, some cast. In general information about the film itself. Maybe it has a category whether it's a premiere or not.

Copy: We must distinguish what is a film from what is a copy. The film is something abstract, it was made at some point in time, it was recorded somehow with the cameras, but what we have are copies. A copy is the film physically. Every unit that is feasible to be delivered and returned. Among its attributes will of course be what film it is, its condition whether it is available or rented, it can be removed if it is lost, or broken, and it may even have a rental history, which will be no more than a collection of rentals.

Renting: A rental can be an object in itself, since we can imagine that it is a complex type of data. It will contain a date of the rental, a date when it must be returned, a date of effective return, it will contain the member who made the rental, and the amount to be paid.

VideoRental: Is the same video rental store really an object? That's a reasonable question, although the answer is obvious. Just as the solar system or the ocean are objects, in this case the video rental store will be an object as well. It's a very particular object, because it contains all the objects of the problem and everything occurs within it. There will be all the members, the films, the copies, the rentals and all other objects that belong to the domain of the problem. Then we must create a class, an instance, and within that instance begin to incorporate all the objects that we need.

The set of classes that result will be left to the reader's discretion, but I will leave a series of questions to invite reflection on some aspects of this problem:

A member rents a movie. Here are two objects, one that sends a message to the other. Where is the action of generating a new rental implemented?

Do you need two classes to distinguish the premieres from the other films?

Do you need two classes to distinguish the categories of members?

Will we need a "Parameters" class, with only one instance where we can record, for example, the prices of the rentals, the number of days each one lasts?

Relationships between classes

There are several ways in which classes relate to each other, and they depend directly on the design that we achieve, and on the way the objects in their instances are related, which are the ones that actually exist in the problem.

The clearest relationship we have seen so far is that of inheritance. Within this type of relationship, class is related to another because it is a sub-class or a super-class. This type of relationship is independent of the lifetime that the objects within the problem have. It is an abstract construction that we make in order to achieve an efficient design.

There are other types of relationships, which "unintentionally" appear in our designs, and which do affect the lifetime of the objects within the problem.

As we saw from the beginning, an object can be built by other objects, and that creates unavoidable links. We can say that some objects participate in the formation of others, and there are also objects whose lifetime is closely related to the lifetime of others. In the example of the receipt we can observe both cases.

Aggregation

There is a relationship of aggregation between classes, when the existence of an object contained in another, does not depend on the existence of the first.

We can see that the receipt can be paid in different ways, and that is reflected in the attribute "payment". There is a relationship between "paymentsOfAReceipt" and "PayingInstrument". But the payment instruments does not depend at all on the existence or not of a receipt, so these objects participate in another, but their existence is not compromised.

Composition

Something different happens when two classes are related through their composition. If one class has a compositional relationship with another, the existence of its objects depends on the existence of others. For example, payment instruments of a receipt and lines are necessary objects for a receipt, but if the receipt for some reason disappears, so do its means of payment and lines.

Conclusions

Throughout these pages, I have tried to give to you a guided tour through the object-oriented paradigm, trying to make it a didactic walk, trying not to depart from the original ideas that defined this way of observing reality, and therefore of solving problems.

The objective of the object-oriented paradigm is to minimize the distance between the problem, its interpretation and solution.

In the beginning of programming, when languages were only very low level, there was a long way to go from the observed problem to the machine code, written in assembler language for example.

Here we can see a program to multiply two numbers, with a lot of restrictions:

```
ORG 100h
MOV AL, 200 ; AL = 0C8h
MOV BL, 4
MUL BL ; AX = 0320h (800)

RET
```

That's a long way from the current A*B, which is much closer to us.
Paradigms and languages aim to move us away from machines and their complexities and

towards human thinking, with the goal of making us more productive. Every translation process, whatever it may be, consumes time and energy. The farther the language of the messenger is from the receiver understanding, the more energy is needed.

Among the existing paradigms, with real, effective and efficient practical application, I consider that nowadays, the object-oriented paradigm is the one that best achieves the objective of shortening the distances between problems and their solutions.

www.ingramcontent.com/pod-product-compliance
Lightning Source LLC
Chambersburg PA
CBHW070435220526
45466CB00004B/1693